MW01599683

Finding the One

A CHRISTIAN MAN'S GUIDE TO MARRIAGE

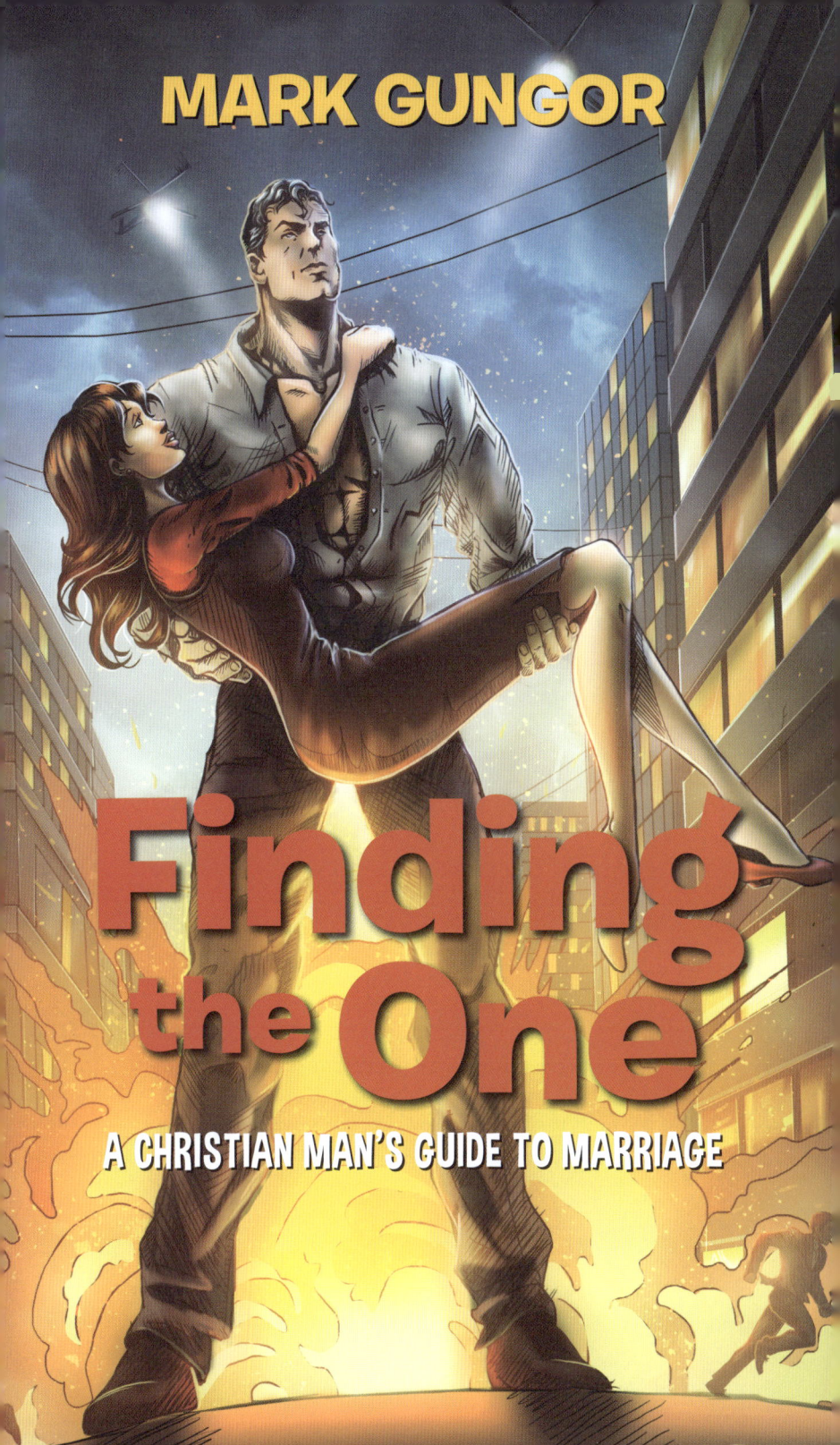

Finding the One – A Christian Man's Guide to Marraige
By Mark Gungor

Book cover illustration by Martina Fačková
Book and cover design by Debbie Bishop

Special thanks to Diane Brierley, Joe Grier and Mary Seipel
for contributing their time and effort in the writing of this book.

For information, address inquiries to: info@laughyourway.com

www.markgungor.com

Scripture quotations taken from The Holy Bible, New International Version [R]
NIV [R] Copyright [C] 1973, 1978, 1984, 2011 by Biblica, Inc. [TM]
Used by permission. All rights reserved worldwide.
Comic balloon page vector designed by winkimages / Freepik
abstract-background-with-dots-that-make-up-a-circle_904973.htm designed by Freepik

Printed in China

To all the guys who are wasting the best years of their lives just...waiting.

Finding the One

A CHRISTIAN MAN'S GUIDE TO MARRIAGE

Contents

Chapter
One

It's About Finding and Being Found

I was speaking at a church in South Africa, talking about how single people need to be proactive and intentional if they want to marry. Immediately after the service a young man came up to me with a text book from a local Bible college he was attending. He opened it up and pointed to a particular paragraph that read:

> *God has ordained a special woman for each man, and it is the responsibility of that man to seek God so that woman can be revealed in his life.*

The young Bible student looked up at me and asked, "Is this true?" I replied very simply, "It is not."

There is no more inaccurate and unbiblical information being passed around the Christian world today than the idea that "God has one special person for everyone." This concept is wholly unsupported in New Testament teaching and only vaguely hinted at in a singular Old Testament reference where Abraham's servant prayed that God would lead him to "the one" when he was trying to find a relative for Isaac to marry. This "help me find the one" prayer was prayed by an unnamed servant, 650 years before Moses gave the most basic Ten Commandments, i.e. a time when people knew very little about God and how he works. Amazingly, that one aberration in the scriptures is what most singles are drawn to today, and for one very clear reason: It supports their foolish, Hollywood-inspired delusions.

The idea that there is "one special person" does not come from the scriptures, but from the secular concept of a "soul mate." Sadly, over the last 2,000 years the church has been all too quick to adopt pagan concepts and repackage them with titles palatable to the Christian community. But putting a pretty bow on a dog turd doesn't change it into a diamond – it is still a dog turd.

The Bible never teaches us to find *"the one."* Oh, it records a "find the one" prayer by a clueless servant – again, 640 years *before* the Ten Commandments – but it never *teaches* us to pray for "the one." And there is a huge difference between what the Bible records (there are all kinds of crazy things people did that is recorded) and what the Bible *teaches.*

When *teaching* about having a wife, the Old Testament uses words like FIND, TAKE and GET. And in the New Testament (the part of the Bible we are to follow most closely) the Apostle Paul clearly taught that marriage was a CHOICE. Read 1 Corinthians Chapter 7 in its entirety. When Paul discusses whether or not to get married, nowhere – not even once – does he say, "Ask God for *the one*" or "Seek God so that He will show you *the one*" or "Just wait on the Lord to bring you *the one*" or any of the other numerous unbiblical pieces of advice that is handed out in churches today.

Solomon, the wisest man who ever lived, penned these words...

> *A wife of noble character is her husband's crown,*
> *But a disgraceful wife is like decay in his bones.*
>
> – Proverbs 12:4

Wait a minute! If God pre-ordains who you will marry, then why would Solomon warn about the kind of woman to choose?

Stop and think about it for a minute. If God truly ordained one person for everyone, all it would take is for one person to get it wrong and the whole thing falls apart anyway.

I mean, if Bob is supposed to marry Juliet, but marries Sarah instead – what is Juliet supposed to do? Now she marries Jack, who was supposed to marry Carmen – well, what is Carmen supposed to do now? Then Carmen marries Fred, who was supposed to marry Wilma...now you have no Flintstones!

And if the church *truly* believed the teaching that "God has ordained ONE SPECIAL PERSON for everyone" – what are we to do with new converts who are already married? If we *truly* believed in the idea of one ordained "soul mate" for everyone, then as soon as married people committed their lives to Christ we would have to insist that they get a divorce (because I'm pretty sure they weren't following "the Lord" when they were dating) and tell them to start seeking God for *"the one."* Can you imagine the destruction of homes and the devastation of children? Christianity would be a curse in the earth instead of a blessing.

Another fallacy is the idea that "God will BRING you a spouse." False, because other than with the creation of Eve in the Garden of Eden, there is no other example of God *bringing* anyone for anybody to marry.

Finally, there is the very spiritual sounding, but equally unsound advice that "God will tell you who to marry." (Apparently, the Apostle Paul didn't know about this one either.) I can tell you with full certainty that there is NO example in the Bible of God ever telling anybody to marry anyone.

The closest you can get is when an angel appeared to Joseph in a dream about taking Mary as his wife. But read it: the angel never tells him to marry her – he just said, "Don't be afraid." Besides, by this point Joseph had already chosen Mary. He was just freaking out because of Mary's unexplained pregnancy.

There are times in the Old Testament when God told someone to get married, but then he never told them *who* to marry. Like when God told Hosea the prophet to marry a prostitute, but never told him which prostitute, he just said, "Pick one."

So, the question becomes: Why doesn't the Bible teach that there is one special person to marry and instead *warns* us to pick wisely? Because a successful marriage is not about finding the right person (though you want to pick the best you can) – a successful marriage is about doing the right things. Period.

You see, the Apostle Paul knew that the principles of Christianity – the principles of love, patience, kindness, forgiveness, long suffering (which means suffering for a looooong time) – these principles are so powerful and life-changing that you could literally take any two people in the world *who live by these principles*, put them together, and they would have a happy and successful marriage. That is why it is so important to live by these principles and to find someone else who does the same.

It isn't about a magical "who," it's about the Godly principles.

Chapter Two

True Happiness

OK, let's start with the basics...what is marriage really for in the first place? Let's start with what it isn't...

Marriage was never designed to be a vehicle to make you happy. This is a major problem for many Christian women who want to find a husband. But the mere notion that there is a man somewhere out there who will meet all the needs of her heart and soul is, well...patently absurd. Let me be clear: There is not a man on earth that can meet all the emotional needs of a woman.

Good grief, no wonder so many married women are incredibly miserable. They heard from some preacher or read on some Christian website that "a man should meet all the emotional needs of his wife." Then they get married, ram a straw into their new groom's head and aggressively start to suck the very life force out of him. "Meet all my needs! Meet all my needs!" This leaves both the groom and bride in a bad place. He is exhausted and feels like a failure, and she gets angry and bitter because he is not living up to some ridiculous standard that doesn't even exist in the real world.

If you are a devout Christian you should already know this one, undeniable truth: God is the only one who can truly meet all the needs of your heart and soul. Remember God's big top ten? The one that says, "Thou shall not have any other gods before me?"

Here is another shocker: Marriage was not created to make you emotionally healthy. It is imperative that you are emotionally healthy *before* you get married – not after. Don't go running off into marriage as an emotionally wounded duck and expect that the "magic of marriage" will fix you. It won't. Get healthy first.

And while we are at it, you need to know that a wife is not a cure for low self-esteem. Don't look to marriage as a cure for deeply held emotional flaws. If anything, marriage will likely expose those flaws – not cover and heal them. I describe this in my book *Laugh Your Way to a Better Marriage*...

In a way, marriage is the great revealer, because you're living in very close quarters. If you ever want to get to know people, go camping with them for a week. Not only will you get to know them, they will get to know you. Somehow who we really are starts to poke out whenever we get close to others over an extended period of time. How we act under pressure in unguarded moments is always telling. Most of us are pretty good at covering up our negative parts under normal conditions; we even fool ourselves into thinking we are better than we are. But close relationships rat us out. This is especially true in marriage.

Most are not comfortable with marriage being a revealer; we want marriage to be a cover. We don't go into marriage to face ourselves; we get married to get away from ourselves, to camouflage who we are.

Ever walk past a mirror and are shocked or mortified by what you see? Your hair standing up in a weird way, your slip showing, your fly open, egg stuck in your teeth? Mirrors can be real lifesavers. Had it not been for that mirror, you may have gone the entire day looking ridiculous.

Marriage is a mirror. By living so closely with another human being, you start to get a picture of what you really look like. You start to see where you need to adjust and change. This is why marriage is so effective at making people's lives more rich and productive – if they adjust to the needed changes. Unfortunately, many expect marriage to be something that makes them look better, not something that reveals where they don't look so good. Additionally, rather than see where we need to change, we opt to project our own negative images on our spouses and point out where they need to change: She is so irritating...he is such a lazy slob...I don't want to act this way, but she brings out the worst in me.

According to a 2009 study detailed in the April 5 issue of the journal *Motivation and Emotion*, researchers found a direct connection between how happy people looked in their college yearbooks and their likelihood of divorce later in life. The researchers rated people's smile intensity from 1 to 10 and then went and interviewed those people, now later in life. **None of the people who fell within the top 10 percent of smile strength had divorced,** while within the bottom 10% of smilers, almost one in four had had a marriage that ended.

Are you seeing this? In this study of just

regular people – not devout religious people, not preachers and their wives, not dedicated Bible students, but regular people – **none** of the people with good smiles had experienced a divorce. How is that possible? **Because they were already happy!!** They didn't need a husband or a wife to fill some empty hole in them. The study went on to say that the correlation was so strong, you could literally predict a person's chance of divorce later in life even from the photos of them as children. That is absolutely fascinating!!

Now, that is not to say if you have a lousy smile you are relationally doomed. Even if you have no teeth at all, you can still have a good marriage – as long as you are the kind of person who is already happy and content. This is not really about smiles – it is about internal joy and happiness.

Want a great marriage that will last a lifetime? Get and stay emotionally healthy. Don't look to marriage to fix you if you are a mess.

Look, if you are a lonely, empty, miserable soul, do everyone a favor and stay single. Because a lonely, empty, miserable soul that marries just remains a lonely, empty, miserable soul. Marriage was never intended to fix that.

So, what is marriage really about? It's about doing life with someone – period. The scriptures tell us that two are better than one...

> *Two are better than one,*
> *because they have a good return*
> *for their labor:*
> *If either of them falls down,*
> *one can help the other up.*
> *But pity anyone who falls*
> *and has no one to help them up.*
> *Also, if two lie down together,*
> *they will keep warm.*
> *But how can one keep warm alone?*
> *Though one may be overpowered,*
> *two can defend themselves.*
> *– Ecclesiastes 4:9-12*

Actual facts support what scripture says. According to the book, ***The Case for Marriage***, researchers reported that married people are healthier, make more money, enjoy life more and literally live longer than their single counterparts. In short – two are better than one.

Marriage is about doing life. Having a family. Paying bills. Changing diapers. Cleaning toilets. Making dinner. Maintaining a house. Fixing the car. Mowing the lawn. Holding each other up during times of adversity. Going to church. Volunteering and serving in your community.

But if you look at that list, the truth is – you can do all of that alone – even raising a family. There is nothing on that list that a single person couldn't do. Then why marry? Because everything on that list becomes easier, better, more fulfilling and longer lasting when you make the journey with a spouse.

Chapter
Three

Everything
Is Fair Game

I received an email from a woman who was bitterly complaining that her husband had a strange obsession with collecting beer cans. Every time he came across a can representing a different brew that was not part of his collection, he would quickly grab it and take it home. She said there were stacks of these empty beer cans all over the house and that she just couldn't take it anymore. She was going to file for divorce, but wanted to know what I thought first.

"Was he collecting these beer cans when you were first dating him?" I asked.

"Yes."

"So, you knew about this in advance?"

"Yes."

Uuuuugh!!! The people who marry someone who does objectionable things that they KNEW they did BEFORE they married them, and then complain bitterly about it later, drive me crazy!! The time to address these issues is *before* the marriage vows are exchanged – not after.

Another person told me that they had had enough and was leaving their spouse because he smoked all the time.

"Were they smoking when you were dating them?"

"Yes."

Uuuuuugh!!

Look, when you are dating somebody and absolutely hate something they continually do... stop dating them!!

Oh, I know, I know...you are under the delusion that the power of the marriage covenant will change them. You think that as soon as you say, "I do," magical powers will descend from the mountain tops and you will now be able to reshape their behavior to your will. But it won't.

I repeat, when you are dating a person and you absolutely hate what they continually do...stop dating them!! Or shut up and accept the behavior.

A big complaint among Christians is that they are dissatisfied with the spiritual state of their spouse. They wanted to marry a deeply spiritual and devout person who will boldly lead them to the throne of grace every day. Instead, they marry a person who never reads their Bible, avoids going to church and refuses to even say grace at the dinner table.

And you couldn't see all this *before* you married?

"But Pastor, she told me she was truly devout."

And you accepted that at face value? Really??

When you were dating her, did she go to church all the time – even when you were unable to go? Did you ever catch her reading a Bible on her own? Did you ever hear her say, "I'm fasting today, so I can't go with you to lunch?" What did she do when the offering basket was passed around?

(This is almost always a dead giveaway.) Did she freely give to the Kingdom of God or did she have to start doing Lamaze breathing techniques, since for her to give money was akin to giving birth? Did you ask her if she tithes? (Yep, that means giving 10 percent of your money to the church.) Generally, only very, very devout people tithe.

"Are you saying I can only marry a very deeply devout woman?"

Certainly not. Just don't marry a woman who is not very devout and later complain that she is not very devout.

The key to finding a successful mate is having your eyes open. Use your brain. Think clearly. Don't over-spiritualize. Quit trying to divine "God's intent for you." Marriage is *your* choice – not *His*. Choose wisely.

Everything is fair game when you are dating.

▶ Is there something in her history you find disturbing?

▶ You can't stand her mother?

▸ She has emotional problems?

▸ Does she always gossip about others?

▸ She doesn't use deodorant?

▸ Is she always dark, moody and depressed?

▸ Does she yell and scream at the other drivers while driving? (Anger issues??)

I had a guy write me once who was really struggling in his marriage. He said he married a woman who used to be a prostitute. She had given her life over to Christ and, after dating her for a while, they married. He wrote me:

"I'm having a really tough time with her past."

"NOW you have a hard time with her past?!? You couldn't think this through BEFORE you married the girl!?!"

Uuuugh...

What really irritates me is when these same men who claim, "God told me to marry her" are ready to divorce her because of one reason or another. What happened to "God?" Boy, do they back pedal on that one. Apparently, God couldn't see what was going to happen down the road.

"The Lord has changed his plan for me."
– **Read:** "I made a terrible decision and I'm too arrogant and proud to admit it."

"God wants me to go in a new direction."
– **Read:** "I like to make up God's will to suit my fancy."

"My wife has hardened her heart to the Lord's will."
– **Read:** "She won't do what I tell her to do and I am always right."

What the guy won't admit is that he was just plain wrong and made a very, very bad choice. What he can't admit is that God doesn't actually tell you who to marry. What he can't admit is that he let his emotions cloud his judgment.

And let me give one more crucial piece of advice here: You should marry someone you actually like and get along with. Sound silly? You have no idea how many times dating couples have asked me for advice to help with their screwed-up relationships. But I always decline. The reason is this: If you need relationship counseling BEFORE you marry – you need to break it off. Marriage counseling is one thing. Dating counseling is just plain stupid. If you and the person you are dating are a mess – end it.

And one thing that truly baffles me is this: People seem to be more committed to their dating relationship than they are to their marriage. No matter what you tell them about what a bad dating match they are in, they refuse to listen. Come hell or high water they will not give up on their girlfriend. But three years into the marriage it seems no matter what you tell them, they are ready to divorce her. This is insane!! The time to end it is BEFORE you say "I do", not AFTER.

I implore you: Have your eyes open. Use your brain. Think clearly. If she does things that you find intolerable while dating her – dump her and move on.

Look for Character

I f you are relatively young, this may come as a surprise to you: Life is hard. If you are older, you no doubt have already become acquainted with this painful fact.

Look, life is really, really, really hard...even for people of faith. Jesus pulled no punches...

"In this world you will have trouble" –
John 16:33

Don't be shocked when life turns dark and things get crazy.

I tell this story in my book, *The BeAttitudes of Marriage...*

The alarm went off at 6:45. I had just flown back from doing one of my Laugh Your Way to a Better Marriage seminars the evening before and struggled to wake up as I needed to get ready to preach four times at our church in Green Bay that Sunday morning.

I looked over at my wife, Debbie, to see how she was doing. She had just started doing chemotherapy to treat the breast cancer they had recently discovered and she was not tolerating it well. They would give her one drug after another to counter the negative effects of some other drug. She found it difficult to sleep at night, but seemed to be resting nicely as I climbed out of bed. I grabbed some appropriate reading materials as I made my way back into the bathroom for my morning "meditations." I closed the door as I entered the bathroom and then closed the second door to the "reflective" room (i.e. sitting on the can).

    Down the stairs in the basement was where one of my younger brothers was staying. He had moved in with us after his wife kicked him out of their home. He needed a place to stay while he was sorting things out. Our family is of Latino descent and Latinos rarely go homeless – we just move in with a relative. Fortunately for most of us, there always seems to be several to choose from. Being the closest and most available, he moved in with us. We called him our basement troll.

    Understandably, his state of affairs was having a very negative affect on his psyche. He was falling further and further into a deep depression. I had yelled at him the night before that he needed to snap out of it. (Apparently, yelling at the depressed is not particularly helpful – who knew??) Unbeknownst to us, he had gone days without sleeping and was on the verge of a manic episode. That morning he snapped and became delusional. He walked up the stairs and started engaging in a heated conversation with me in the kitchen. Only problem: I wasn't in the kitchen – I was still "meditating."

My wife woke up and heard my brother in the kitchen threatening to shoot me. She thought it was unusual that I was not talking back since I am famous for having an opinion about most everything (whether or not I know what I'm talking about never seems to hinder me), and she concluded that I must be frozen in fear. She quickly grabbed her phone and called 911.

"My husband is trapped in the kitchen and his brother is threatening to shoot him!"

"Alright ma'am, the police are on

their way."

As my wife stayed huddled in our bedroom, unsure of what would happen next, I walked out of the bathroom wearing nothing but a t-shirt and a smile.

"What are you doing here?!" she whispered loudly. (Apparently, wives can still yell at you even while they are whispering. Again, who knew??)

"Well...I live here."

"I thought you were in the kitchen with your brother!! He was threatening to shoot you! The police just arrived and want us to come out with our hands up!!!"

I thought to myself, "Oh no, the drugs have caused her to go crazy!!" I stared at her in disbelief.

"We need to go outside!!" she stressed.

"I'm naked."

"For heaven's sake, get dressed!!!!" Again, the whispering was rather intense.

By now my brother had gone

back into the basement, so when I came out of the bedroom, having properly girded my loins of course, there was no brother. I truly thought my wife was losing it. I looked outside and sure enough, there stood a couple of Green Bay's finest, guns at the ready, waving at us to quickly run to them.

"Oh good grief!" I thought to myself. I still thought my wife was imagining the entire conversation as a result of her drugged up state.

We quickly ran over to the officers as my wife repeated what she had heard. After hearing her story, the officer looked at me. I paused. I looked at my wife. I paused. I looked at the police. I paused. I looked back at her.

"Look, my wife is going through chemo and taking all kinds of drugs and she may be hallucinating..." I continued as I tried to explain to the police why we were in this ridiculous scenario.

Now, you should see the kind of look your wife gives you while you are explaining to the police that she is likely not in her right mind. Strangely enough, it is much louder than even the whisper yelling. But what was I to do. There was no brother in the kitchen. I was clearly not in conversation with him. I never heard anything. She was taking a lot of drugs. What would you think??

Just then, several squad cars zoomed in, one after another, lining our quiet neighborhood with pretty blinking lights. I watched in horror as officers quickly surrounded our house, their guns pulled and ready. One of the officers yelled over, "He just called in to the police and said he had the house rigged for explosives and was going to blow it up!!" Apparently, our basement troll had indeed completely lost it and was now calling emergency numbers to threaten everyone he could.

31

I snapped my head over to look at my wife to witness her eyes piercing through my soul as she growled, "I told you so..."

My mind wanted to ponder all the ways my wife would kill me later for telling the police that she was a nut case, but instead I had this horrifying thought: WHAT WOULD THE NEIGHBORS THINK???!!!! All they had to do is look out their windows and witness the local pastor's house surrounded by police, guns at the ready, and the road covered with cars that were blinking red and blue. I could imagine my elderly neighbor saying to his wife, "I knew that man was unstable. They're probably operating a crack house over there..."

My thoughts were broken as a police officer looked me squarely in the face and with all sincerity asked of me, "Sir, do you have any explosives in the house?!"

"What??!!" I retorted. "Who has explosives in their house????!!!!"

"Sir, he has threatened to blow the house up."

"Oh for heaven's sake," having finally gotten a sense of just what was going on, "it's just my brother in the basement. Clearly, he has had a mental lapse due to his depression. Just go down there and get him!"

Ahhhh, yes...just another day here on Earth.

It may come as a shock to you younger readers, but life on earth is not heaven. We live in a fallen, sinful, selfish, violent, angry and cursed world. It's really, really, really hard living on this planet.

People often tell me that they are looking for someone they are compatible with. Sadly, they don't even know what the word means. The word "compatible" comes from the Latin word "compati" which literally means: to suffer with. Being compatible is not about two people who like all the same things and always feel the same way about everything. There is a different word for that: **Delusional.**

That is why when you are dating, you should be looking for someone of character – someone you can "suffer with." Don't get caught up in how "cute" a girl is. Character will last you a life time. Sexy has a shelf life.

▸ What are you going to do if the doctor tells you about the tumor he found in her breast?

▸ What are you going to do if you lose your job?

▸ What are you going to do if she keeps having miscarriage after miscarriage?

▸ What are you going to do if your child has physical or learning disabilities?

A woman of character will always be there

for you. A woman without character (even if she is really, really good looking) will abandon you – either emotionally or literally.

Life is hard. Look for someone you can do life with – someone you can "suffer with."

And when you are dating a girl, don't just look at how she acts – look at how she reacts. Hey, anybody can "act." It doesn't mean that is who they really are. That is why they call it "acting."

But reacting. Ahhhh...that is hard to fake. It is in the reacting that you start to see a person's true character.

▸ How does she react when something doesn't go her way?

▸ How does she react when another car cuts in front of her?

▸ How does she react when her parents tell her something she doesn't want to hear?

▸ How does she react when things go badly for her at work?

Look at the reactions of her life. Study them carefully. Can you live with them? Remember this: You will date the "act," but you will marry the **"react."**

Chapter
Five

Get
a Clue

W hen my son Phil was a young man, just out of high school, already with a goal to find a girl to marry, he called me from Tulsa, Oklahoma.

"Dad, what should I look for in a girl? I mean like…physically?"

I replied, "As long as she has boobs and a nice smile, you'll be in good shape!"

Talk about an area of life where guys are missing the boat today! So many guys are overlooking beautiful, wonderful girls that would make them so happy, because they have their sights set on a "10." You know – a super babe with a body like a swimsuit model, a face like a Revlon

37

girl, and a brain like Madam Curie. But boys – get a clue!!

I actually believe the huge amount of romantic films available today at a click of a button is having an entirely negative impact on both men and women by creating unbelievably, unrealistic expectations.

Just a few decades ago, people didn't see movie after movie after movie. Because if we wanted to see a movie, WE ACTUALLY HAD TO GO TO THE MOVIE THEATER. But today, click and stream and stream and click and you can watch five romantic flicks in a single night. And don't kid yourself – this has an impact on you. Every time you see that perfectly gorgeous girl kissing the boy in that movie – you picture her kissing you. Come on – some of you have already fantasized over the ridiculous cover on this book. Hour after hour after grueling hour you view and fantasize – and make no mistake – it affects your perspective.

Is a guy today interested in that cute girl at church? Nah. She doesn't look anything like a supermodel. What about the brunette in his class that is always smiling and laughing? No way. She would never be on the cover of *Sports Illustrated.*

Really?? Dude, have you looked in the mirror?!? Get a clue!!

I have spent time with so many young men who are literally waiting for a babe like they've fantasized about in the movies. The problem is, these guys are no prized pigs!! Seriously, if they were literally pigs at a fair, no way would they get a blue ribbon. They probably wouldn't even get a participation trophy. And they ignore the other pretty girls in their church because they think they are going to get a super babe?! Really???

Hey, the girls have the same problem. They watch more of those stupid movies than you do. And they, too, fantasize that the hunky boy in the movie is actually kissing them. And you just do not measure up to that handsome movie star image that has been seared into her brain.

Step back a minute. Look at all the happily married guys in your church. Did they marry super-babes? Not hardly. But they have what you don't: A woman that loves them, that makes love to them, that has babies with them, that have nice homes with them, and in general, have really, really nice lives.

You, on the other hand, are still living in your mom's basement, waiting for Ms. Perfect to fall into your arms. Here's the thing – Ms. Perfect already saw you coming...and moved to the other side of the street! Get a clue!!

Ease up on the perfect hair and the perfect teeth and the perfect skin and the perfect boobs with the perfect butt that you have stuck in your head.

Whenever I speak to singles groups, I always am stunned at the apparent stupidity that is right before them. There they sit – 400 available single men and women, listening to me...because NOBODY CAN FIND ANYONE TO MARRY!! Really? How about the girl sitting next to you??

But no. Combine the standard for physical perfection with the desire of spiritual maturity and the necessity of intellectual purity connected to the right height, hair and complexion and then... there is just no one to marry. Sigh...

Get a clue!!

When I was young it was awfully simple: You found a pretty girl who liked you back. Done. She didn't need to look like a movie star, compete with a swimsuit model or solve mysteries like a rocket scientist.

A) She was a girl with all the right parts in all the right places,

B) She was nice,

C) When you showed interest in her, she showed interest back.

Done.

But no, not today. Today most guys reach for heights that, quite frankly, they will never attain. Eventually they do get a clue and settle for a normal, wonderful woman. But by then, they have wasted all of their 20s and half their 30's…and for what? Nothing.

And we have skipped over one of the most

poisonous influences of all: Porn. Guys who look at porn REALLY get a twisted reality in their heads. They stare at the handful of women in the world that look like that. Yet that unattainable, finite minority of women with absolutely perfect bodies becomes their goal – a goal they will never, ever, ever reach.

Come on guys, get a clue!!

Until young men break the cycle of unrealistic expectations, the joy of marriage will continue to elude them.

Chapter Six

But What if There Is No One Available?

I received an email from a woman living in the Caribbean Islands who was rather irritated after hearing me tell people that if they want to have a mate, they need to go find one.

She wrote, "I am on a small island in the Caribbean and there are no men available. You say God won't just bring me a man and that I have to find one. What am I supposed to do?"

My answer: **MOVE!!**

Good grief, you either want to get married or you don't. Living on an island where there are no men is probably not a good plan.

I get the same thing from guys who attend very small churches. "I attend a very small church and there are no women available. What am I supposed to do?"

Go to a bigger church!!

Look, if you are trying to catch a fish, but you are sitting at a small pond with no fish...you need to move to a different body of water. Ideally, a really big one. Then your chances are better.

Or you can listen to the flawed advice given by so many Christians, "Don't worry, God will bring you a wife." Then you can join the countless hordes of Christian men who never marry.

Imagine this scenario: A man is sitting alone in a chair, tears of frustration streaming down his face. You ask him what is wrong. He replies, "I am very near sighted and I can't find my glasses." You tell him not to worry and that you would be more than happy to help him find his glasses. "No! No!" he protests, "I am waiting for God to bring me my glasses."

Or this scenario: A man complains bitterly of his dire financial situation. They have cut off his electricity and he has been served an eviction notice on his apartment. He is unemployed and has been praying and fasting that he will find a job. You ask, "Where have you looked for a job?" Confidently and boldly he perks up in response, "Oh, I am not looking for a job. I am trusting that God will bring me a job!"

Your response to the previous scenarios are either a) slap them or b) call the looney squad. Yet this is precisely the way so many Christian singles act – mostly due to very flawed teaching and poor, unbiblical advice.

And here is another problem that we have in many churches: It's not that there isn't anyone available – there just isn't anyone available that "turns their crank." This happens a lot with young people who grow up in our churches. We unwittingly create an atmosphere of familiarity amongst our youth and cause them not to be interested in each other. I think it is a bad idea when we have our young men and women spend so much time with each other in youth groups, Bible studies, outreaches, mission trips, etc.... We succeed in destroying all sexual tension between them (and it is sexual tension that draws a man and woman together). So instead of maintaining a healthy degree of separation, we destroy all mystery between these young men and women so they view each other more as brothers and sisters than potential mates.

The best possible scenario is that young people who grow up in our churches end up marrying someone from their church. That way, we know what they have been taught all those years, they share the same spiritual values and we know their families – many which are our personal friends.

But no – we destroy all of that by sticking the boys and girls so close together that all dating interest is obliterated.

Is he now interested in the cute readhead in the Youth group? No.

"Ewww, that would be like marrying my sister!"

Sadly, the guys in church are not interested in the girls they know – they want a girl they don't know. All you have to do is watch what happens when a new girl comes into the church. All the guys are fascinated by her. "Ooooo...look how cute she is. I wonder what she is like?"

Of course, they are enamored with her – they haven't seen her act like a whiney, emotionally draining, pre-menstrual nightmare yet. But hey, when a guy dates a girl he dosen't know, he can place on her all the fantasies and delusions he carries.

How about we stop sticking our young men and women so closely together that they lose all romantic interest in each other? How about maintaining some mystery and attraction? And how about dating someone you actually do know instead of being sucked in by the siren song of mystery?

Listen to Your Friends and Family

The common encouragement given to many young people is this: *Follow your heart.* This, however, is deeply flawed advice.

The heart (which represents your emotions) has been getting people into relational nightmares for thousands of years.

The heart is deceitful above all things and beyond cure. Who can understand it?

– Jeremiah 17:9

"But I have to be honest with how I feel."

Really? I have never understood this line of thinking. Your emotions can go up and down from one minute to the next. Why would you be honest with the most dishonest part of you? Only in relationships are we so incredibly foolish. If there is one thing you can do that will virtually guarantee failure in life, it is this: Follow your feelings.

People who are successful in life never follow their feelings. Students who study don't ask themselves if they feel like studying. World class musicians never ask themselves if they feel like practicing scales six hours a day. Entrepreneurs never ask themselves if they feel like working eighteen hour days.

Consider Biblical heroes. I doubt Shadrach, Meshach and Abednego felt like being thrown into the fiery furnace. I'm pretty sure Daniel did not want to be cast into the den of lions. We know Moses did not want to go talk to Pharaoh. And Jonah got in big trouble trying to run away from God. You can bet the family farm that Paul didn't want to be beaten and thrown into jail. And if you think about it, even Jesus didn't want to go to the cross. Remember his prayer in the garden? "Father, if there is any possible way, let this cup pass from me..."

The writer of Hebrews gives us a great summary of people who probably didn't feel like doing what they had to do...

> There were others who were tortured, refusing to be released so that they might gain an even better resurrection. Some faced jeers and flogging, and even chains and imprisonment. They were put to death by stoning; they were sawed in two; they were killed by the sword.
>
> They went about in sheepskins and goatskins, destitute, persecuted and mistreated – the world was not worthy of them. They wandered in deserts and mountains, living in caves and in holes in the ground.
>
> – Hebrews 11:35-38

Do you know why successful people don't listen to their feelings? Because their feelings would scream, "Don't do it!!" Why? Because being successful requires sacrifice and nobody *feels* like sacrificing.

What is it that makes people think when it comes to dating that feelings must somehow be heeded? Married life is loaded with things no one wants to do.

But despite these warnings, dating is a highly emotional state and your emotions can cloud your head.

"So how can I sort things out and know the right things to do?"

Listen to your friends and family and mentors. They will see things you don't see. Trust their judgments and insights. They know you. They love you. They want the best for you.

Hollywood, romance novels and television shows are filled with dramatic stories of how friends and family get in the way of true love. In these stories, it is only by ignoring friends and family and following the heart that true love is realized.

Just look at Romeo and Juliet! Their families tried to keep them apart, but they followed their hearts instead. Yeah...and they both wound up dead. They probably should have listened to their friends and families.

> *Plans fail for lack of counsel, but with many advisers they succeed.*
> – Proverbs 15:22

But let me be clear: When someone gives you advice, it just a way for you to see and hear a different perspective. It's a way to perhaps consider things you might not have considered before. It allows you to reflect on insights separate from your own feelings and emotions. It does not, however, mean you are obligated to do what they say. In the end, you must make your own decisions. Marriage is always *your* choice. You just want to be sure you choose wisely.

And allow me to give some advice to those of you who are younger: You need to honor your parents, but you don't need to obey them. If you are six years old you need to obey them, but if you are a grown man, you are responsible for your own decisions. If you love someone and want to marry her and your parents disapprove, it just means they disapprove. You will want to listen to their input about your decision, but in the end, it is your decision. You can *respectfully* and *honorably* acknowledge their disapproval, but you have every right before God to marry whomever you wish, whenever you wish.

This is particularly important today because so many well-meaning parents have developed such a negative attitude towards the institution of marriage. Maybe it's because their own marriage is bad. Perhaps it is due to all the negative propaganda about young marriage that is in our secular culture today. I don't know. All I know is that marriage is an honorable institution established by God for the benefit of human beings. If your parents disapprove of your plan to marry, be sure to listen to their concerns. Be respectful. Be honorable. But make your own decision. As an adult – even a young adult – you are not obligated to "obey" your parents. Children must obey. Adults must honor. And those are two very different things.

Oh, they may threaten not to attend the wedding, pay for your education, cut you out of their will or a myriad of other hurtful steps. But if they do any of that, it is on them – not you. (By the way, all of their disapproval is likely to disappear very quickly when you start giving them grandchildren.)

If I had "obeyed" my parents, I would never have married my wife. They said we were too young, too poor, too ignorant and that it would likely never last. That was over 40 years ago.

Listen to your family and friends. Consider their view points. Try not to be clouded by your emotions and feelings. But in the end, this is your life and your choice. Choose wisely.

Chapter Eight

Extraordinary Measures

People seem to have a very negative impression about online dating. I, on the other hand, don't see the big deal. Marriage is about finding and being found. And since the beginning of time, there is only one way to find things: You look for them.

As long as a man is using his brain and being intentional, I think online dating or most any other form of dating (excluding the new "naked dating") should be acceptable.

"But there are so many trolls and bad people online!!"

Yes, I've seen them. But they seem rather

easy to point out – not sure what the problem is – unless you think online dating will be easy and you are discouraged that it is not. Hey, looking is hard. It is time consuming. It can be frustrating and very inconvenient. But there is no way to substitute trying to find something: You must look.

Then there is the highly-debated subject of dating non-Christians. Debated because the Bible is very clear that a believer should not get tangled up with a non-believer. But I am not advocating any tangling – just looking. Come on, if you can't find a believer as marriage material, look at some of the non-believers in your life.

Take her to dinner. Invite her to church. Let her meet some of your Christian friends. Treat her like a million dollars and don't try to grab her boobs or get into her pants. Who knows if you won't win that girl to Jesus? It doesn't mean you have to marry her. Even if you eventually don't end up together, perhaps you can change her life for eternity.

I was at a conference of Pastors and Missionaries from around the world. Sitting with several of them at dinner, I told them of my thoughts concerning dating non-believers. Two of the pastors starting giggling and their wives had funny smirks of their faces.

"What?"

"Well, that's what we did."

"Seriously?"

One pastor responded, "Yep, I couldn't find anyone I liked, so I saw this one, took her to church, got her saved and married her. That was over 20 years ago."

For some guys, just asking a woman out can be viewed as an "extraordinary measure." It can feel like a huge risk for a guy to put his ego and manhood on the line to even ask a woman out.

What if she says no? He needs to know that he stands a chance with the girl before he'll even consider asking. So how can a guy know?

Look for the green lights.

- ▸ Is she showing more interest in you or is she chattier with you than other guys?

- ▸ Does she seek you out in a group or social situation?

▶ Do you find her smiling at you, laughing at your jokes, making eye contact with you?

▶ What about her body language?

▶ Is she conveying an openness or does she touch your arm or hand during interaction?

Don't wait for the woman to ask you out. Be the man. Be brave. Make the move. If she turns you down – so what? It's not like you're going to lose an eye or something. Despite what you may feel, no guy has ever died from being turned down.

Fear not. You'll be fine.

Chapter Nine

The Power of an Erection

Admit it: You want sex.

If your response to the previous paragraph is, "No I don't!!" then why are you reading this book and why are you considering marriage? Because the New Testament teaches us that if you are not interested in and desire sex, you should just stay single. The Apostle Paul wrote...

Now to the unmarried...I say: It is good for them to stay unmarried, as I do. But if they cannot control themselves, they should marry, for it is better to marry

61

than to burn with passion.

– 1 Corinthians 7:8-9

He also states:

But since sexual immorality is occurring, each man should have sexual relations with his own wife, and each woman with her own husband.

– 1 Corinthians 7:2

Simply put: **Marriage is for sex.**

Few statements cause more revulsion than the statement that declares, "If you want sex, get married."

Secular culture is repulsed by such logic because they have cheapened sex to the point that it means virtually nothing.

In the Kevin Costner movie, *"The Guardian,"* the character played by Ashton Kutcher freely has sex with some chick he meets in a bar. They have sex, of course, because they spent all of ten minutes talking to each other and, as everyone knows, after ten minutes of talking, the only next logical step is to get naked and start fornicating. [Please note sarcasm.]

Anyway, after multiple fornicating romps, Kutcher's character finally asks the girl he has just finished ravishing if she would like to have dinner with him. Her response is, "I don't know if I want to get serious enough for dinner."

WHAT?!?!?!

You can get totally naked, have the man see, feel and have access to any part of your body (apparently that is OK), but DINNER??? No, no, no...that is something that must be considered carefully!!

And that, my friends, is how most secular people view sex. A mere physical activity that is connected to...nothing. Then when they hear the statement: "You should marry for sex," they scoff, howl, mock and ridicule such a statement.

But the other group that has the same visceral, negative response to the very same idea, that marriage is for sex, is Christians. Why? Because they have been told that marriage is about being "one in the spirit," about "being prayer partners," about "deep spiritual intimacy," about "fulfilling a divine destiny," etc... etc... etc... blah... blah... blah... What you don't hear is that marriage is fundamentally about sex. Apparently, for both the secularist and the Christian, sex is too cheap for marriage, but both groups are wrong. Sex is too precious for anything outside of marriage.

When Jesus told his disciples that they could not divorce a woman for any ol' reason they replied:

> "If this is the situation between a husband and wife, it is better not to marry."   – Matthew 19:10

Unfazed by their objection, Jesus replied by reminding them that they either wanted to have sex or they didn't:

> "...there are eunuchs who were born that way, and there are eunuchs who have been made eunuchs by others – and there are those who choose to live like eunuchs for the sake of the kingdom of heaven."
>   – Matthew 19:12

Now for those ignorant of what a eunuch is, let me be plain: It is a man without testicles. When the disciples recoiled at the notion that they couldn't just dump their wives freely as they saw fit, and concluded that it was then "better not to marry," Jesus was literally telling them...

"Hey, some guys are born without a pair, others have their pair taken away from them and there are even some guys who give up their pair willingly so they can serve God without distraction."

Wow...that was pretty cold.

Shorthand: Since men without a pair don't want sex, Jesus said you either want sex or you don't.

Interestingly, the disciples never brought up the subject again.

Only a knave or a fool could read the New Testament and fail to come away with the conclusion that marriage is for sexual fulfillment. Even the Old Testament is full of vibrant sexual imagery when referring to marriage. Just read Solomon's *"Song of Songs."*

Sexual fulfillment is okay. Actually, it is more than okay, for we are sexual beings that have been created for sexual desire and fulfillment. But if you are not interested in sex, please put down this book, stop dating women and get a dog.

Sex is essential for a successful marriage. Sex is the Novocain that makes marriage possible. It draws us to each other, it bonds us to each other, it heals and strengthens us, and not just emotionally. Again from *Laugh Your Way to a Better Marriage*...

> *There are wagonloads of evidence that say sex is great for a person's health. In fact, having sex an average of three times a week is equivalent to running eighty miles a year. Sex increases good hormone production, strengthens bones, improves muscle tone, and loads your system with good cholesterol. Endorphin release, which is nature's aspirin for pain, happens during sex, and makes it a great management tool for the general aches*

and pains that present themselves in our bodies.

The hormone DHEA (dehydroe-piandrosterone), produced by the adrenal glands, is also released just before orgasm. DHEA improves mental awareness, boosts the immune system, inhibits the growth of tumors in the body, and builds bone tissue. In a woman, oxytocin (the "love and cuddle" chemical) is released in huge doses during sex. A woman's estrogen level also increases. Estrogen gives a woman an overall feeling of contentment and calm, aides in memory retention, and affords her a healthier cardiovascular system.

I am appalled by how many pastors and Christian leaders don't understand that sex is central to the marriage covenant. Sex is and always has been a sexual contract. When you say, "I do," it means, "I do you, you do me and we don't do anybody else."

And when I say I am appalled at how many pastors and Christian leaders fail to acknowledge that sex is central to marriage, that is not being totally truthful. The truth is – I am furious!

I continue to be shocked and amazed at how many people tell me a story like this...

"We got married and on our wedding night and honeymoon, I found out that my new wife had no interest in sex. In fact, she was totally opposed to it and refuses to have sex with me."

Some of them have been married for over a decade in a sexless marriage by the time I hear their heartbreaking story. I always ask in bewilderment, "What did your pastor say?!?"

"He said that it's too late – we are married now and we have to just deal with it."

Can there be that much ignorance in the clergy today?!? For thousands of years of human history – even Jewish history where we receive much of our understanding of the

Christian faith – a man and a woman were never considered married until the marriage had been consummated [meaning the couple had sex]. The family *literally* would wait outside the tent or door and wanted to see the soiled bed linens as proof of the consummation before they were considered married. (Gross, right?)

I recently saw a documentary on PBS where they said sex was so important in the marriage of the royalty that state dignitaries and family members would stay in the bedroom, waiting for the king and his new queen to do the deed. They would even offer "suggestions" and "encouragements" to the newly betrothed. (OK, now that is just creepy!!)

So...how on God's green Earth did pastors ever come to the conclusion that people were married just because they said, "I pronounce you Man & Wife"???

Sigh...sometimes it is more than I can bear.

These men of God condemn people to a miserable life of a sexless marriage all because these same men fail to understand the true covenant of marriage.

"But we don't believe in divorce."

For heaven's sake, a divorce is not called for!! This denial of sex by one spouse to the other is the classic moral and legal reason for an annulment. Yes, even in the 21st century, failure to consummate a marriage is grounds for an immediate annulment.

Dear reader, I don't care what any pastor, mentor, religious leader or family member tells you – if on your honeymoon, your bride refuses to have sex with you...YOU GET AN ANNULMENT. Do not go to counseling. Do not talk to doctors. Do not give yourselves to prayer and fasting. Do not pass Go. Do not collect $200. You get an annulment. Game over. Redo. Reset. Period.

And what the heck are these people discussing during their pre-marriage counseling sessions anyway?? You mean to tell me that after hours and hours of pre-marriage counseling, no one ever posited the question, "You guys both want to have sex, right?"

The good news is that most men and women do want sexual intimacy, and the way to a fulfilled, safe and secure sex life is only in the context of marriage.

And I repeat: If you do not sincerely desire sex, please put down this book, stop dating women and get a dog.

Chapter Ten

No "Thinky", No "Touchy"

This is what the Apostle Paul wrote...

"It is not good for a [single] man to touch a woman." – 1 Corinthians 7:1

I call it the "No touchy" rule.

Jesus was even more restrictive. In his sermon on the mount he basically taught: *Don't even think about it* (Matthew 5:28). I call this the "No thinky" rule.

So, when single couples ask me "How far can we go?" I answer, "As long as there is No Thinky and No Touchy, you can go as far as you like."

Let me be brutally clear: When you are dating a woman, you do not touch her breasts and you do not put your hand down her pants to fondle her vagina. AND, she should not be touching your willy either.

Any questions?

Besides, the whole "How far can I go?" question is nonsense. You want to have sex?? Just get married. Then you can have all the sex you want, and in a context that will bring you emotional health, not emotional stupidity.

And here is one of the biggest reasons for waiting until marriage for sex: The single greatest indicator of divorce is not age, money, or education – it is prior sexual activity.

A few years ago Robert Rector and Kirk Johnson of the Heritage Foundation did an analysis of the 1995 *National Survey of Family Growth* and found: "For women 30 or older, those who were monogamous (only one sexual partner in a lifetime) had a divorce rate of only 20 percent. Sleeping with just one extra partner increased that probability to 46 percent. Two extra partners boosted the number to 56 percent. Who would have thought that the price of sleeping with even one premarital partner would lead to divorce for almost half of those who had only one extra tryst?"

Data from the *National Survey of Family Growth* shows: "[Those] who are sexually active prior to marriage faced considerably higher risk of marital disruption than [those] who were virgin[s]."

The very respected *National Health and Social Life Survey*, conducted at the University of Chicago found a marked connection between premarital sex and elevated risk of divorce. "For both genders, we find that virgins have dramatically more stable first marriages..."

Sociologist Jay Teachman examined how both premarital sex and cohabitation affect marriage relationships for women. He found "...that women with more than one intimate relationship prior to marriage have an elevated risk of marital disruption."

Professor Anthony Pail at the University of Iowa found that women who had sex in their teens had roughly double the risk of divorce as those who did not. Interestingly enough, he found that teen girls who experienced their first sexual experience with a young man who would eventually be her husband did not have an elevated risk of divorce. Sadly, few girls who lose their virginity as teens wind up marrying the boy. The vast majority of sexually active teens end up having multiple sexual partners which increases their later risk for divorce.

And the studies go on and on and on…

If you are not a virgin on your wedding day are you doomed to marital failure? Of course not. But it would be foolish to dismiss what science and virtually every culture in the world for thousands of years have known: Pre-marital sex will make you stupid.

I am not saying you have to "group date." You can be alone with her…as long as you are alone in public. What does that mean? It means you can take her to a nice restaurant, have your own table and enjoy your own private conversations – in public.

You can take her for romantic walks – in public.

You can enjoy the latest movies – in a public theater.

Don't go spending time alone in private. If you do, you will inevitably cross lines you should not cross. **Be smart. Do it right.**

Stop Wacking Off!

In my first book, ***Laugh Your Way to a Better Marriage***, I wrote about the absurdity and dangers of masturbation:

> *Stuart Brody of the University of Paisley, UK, and Tillmann Kruger of the Swiss Federal Institute of Technology in Zurich measured blood prolactin levels in male and female volunteers who achieved orgasm while engaging in masturbation versus sexual intercourse in the laboratory. (Boy, you have to wonder what kind of person would volunteer*

to masturbate or have sex in a lab?) To the researchers' surprise, the increase in blood prolactin levels was four hundred percent higher in both sexes after orgasm from sexual intercourse compared with orgasm from masturbation. "This explains why orgasm from intercourse is more satisfying than masturbation," says Brody.

Masturbating is not real sex; it carries one-fourth the impact of real sex. A real orgasm occurs when your body reaches a sexual peak and endorphins are released into your bloodstream and every cell in your body stands up, grabs the hand of the cell next to it, and shouts, "Hallelujah!" The narcotic-like buzz of a real orgasm can last for hours. That is an orgasm. During masturbation, all you experience is a hollow sexual release.

Sex experts, psychologists, and even preachers, however, have gone out of their way to try to convince people they do not have to feel bad about masturbating. My response to that is: You may be able to fool your mind into not feeling bad after masturbating, but you will never be able to fool your body into an actual orgasm. All you will experience is a hollow release that is not equivalent to an orgasm. That is why those who masturbate often report engaging in the activity three, five, even seven times a day – or more. The masturbator must repeat the deed again and again to satisfy his or her sexual need.

Foolishly, serial masturbators are deluded into thinking that multiple ejaculations are a sign of their sexual virility, but they are not. Their bodies know that what is going on is not sex, and if the masturbators ignore their body and continue this activity, they will ultimately pay the price as they condition their bodies to an alternate and inferior form of stimulation.

In his book *"**When Good Men Are Tempted,**"* author Bill Perkins writes:

During a counseling session a woman blurted out, "Bill, Shawn never wants to have sex with me anymore. When we first got married, that was all he wanted to do. Now we only have sex once a month, and that's when I beg him." While meeting alone with me, Shawn told me, "It's just easier to view pornography and masturbate. I've done that for years. It saves me the hassle of dealing with my wife."

I wish I could say Shawn's behavior is unusual. It isn't. Men often prefer sexual gratification without intimacy and self-sacrifice. Obviously, when masturbation drains a person of sexual energy, their spouse will suffer the consequences.

Men and women may think that having lots of hot, lusty, sexually charged masturbatory events centered on fantasy and self-indulgence is a great idea, but the reality does not live up to the promise. I ask guys who are always checking out other women, looking at pornography on the Internet, and sitting around in the dark masturbating (what I lovingly refer to as "yanking on your wanger"), "How's that working for you? Is your sex life pretty good?'

They quickly admit that their sex life stinks.

A man at one of my conferences said he could have sex for hours on end but nothing ever happened. No matter what, he could not achieve an orgasm. He had conditioned his penis through masturbation so that it would not respond to a woman's vagina.

Men (and women) can actually condition their genitals through masturbation. Many men exert much more pressure with their hands than they are likely to experience during intercourse. In doing so, they essentially train themselves to sexually respond to lots of pressure. In its most severe manifestation, delayed ejaculation takes the form of ejaculatory incompetence, a condition where the man can never ejaculate inside the vagina.

Women can suffer the same consequences. I know of many women who find it virtually impossible to respond to a man's penis because they have spent years and years training themselves to respond to their own hands or a vibrator. Women who use vibrators to gratify themselves apart from their husbands need to understand that their husbands will never be able to recreate the sensation that the battery-powered vibrator does.

Let me be clear: I do not have a problem with couples learning about each other's bodies by stimulating each other. I do not have a problem with couples who are separated from each other for extended periods of time talking sexually on the phone or communicating via the Internet and touching themselves as they interact with each other. (Still, not as great as the real thing though.)

My objection is tying masturbation to pornography and to fantasies that create destructive addictions. My objection with masturbation is when it is a solo endeavor, practiced in an imaginary world of unrealistic sexual fantasy. My objection is with men and women who, while living in a home with a real person, choose to ignore that person and "take matters into their own hands." My objection is with lying to teenagers and encouraging them to engage in an activity that is peddled as "good and natural," when it holds the potential to damage their sex lives.

Masturbation is not real sex. It is not great sex. It is not fulfilling sex. It is *a counterfeit experience that can rob you of the joy of real sex. A man should be a lover to his wife, skillfully captivating her heart so she willingly gives her body to him and he can make passionate love to her. A woman should be a lover to her husband, skillfully capturing his heart in passionate love.*

Many women's books and magazines will tell their readers that women need to masturbate to learn what feels good to them and to understand their bodies. But you don't have to do that alone. Husbands and wives should be exploring each other's bodies together to learn what feels good, not going off on a solo adventure. Sex should be a team sport, not an individual competition. Know that just as there are experts out there promoting vibrators and masturbation for women, there are also experts saying that these things will make it more difficult for a woman to achieve orgasm and satisfaction when actually making love with her husband.

Masturbation is the lazy coward's way out. Instead of being a lover to his or her spouse, the masturbator ends up becoming a lover of self.

Ending up as a serial masturbator can be a big danger. I know, I know...you think "I'll stop once I am married." What you don't understand is that you WON'T stop after you are married. The problem of young men damaging and misdirecting their sexual energy cannot be overstated. I continue to hear from heartbroken wives that their husbands would rather masturbate than make love to them. Can you believe it? These guys get so attached to making love to their own hands that they have little to no interest in their wife's vagina.

I was sitting in my office one day when a gorgeous young brunette of 27 years of age knocked on my door. She asked if she could have a few minutes of my time. I assured her it was fine and invited her to take a seat.

"How can I help you?" I queried.

"It's my husband. He hasn't touched my vagina in over a year!"

Now, I must admit. It is not customary for young ladies to come into my office and start discussing their vagina. To say I was taken back for a moment would be an understatement.

"Excuse me?"

"My husband...he hasn't touched my vagina in over a year. I want to have sex with him, but is just not interested. He would rather take things into his own hands."

By this point, I was completely stunned. Here is this drop-dead, gorgeously stunning young woman complaining to me that her husband would much rather masturbate than make love to her. Truth be told, I just couldn't believe her. Surely there was something else going on.

"Have you talked to him about this?"

"Of course, but he doesn't care."

"Do you think he would be willing to come in with you and talk this over with me?" Again, I had to assume there was something I was missing here.

She confidently assured me that she could get him to come back in with her, so we set up another time to meet.

When the time for the meeting arrived, sure enough, here she comes with her husband in tow. He was a big, strong, nice looking young man and seemed very willing to be meeting with me.

I paused for a moment, not really sure how one would jump into such a discussion. "Openly Discussing the Vagina" is not a class offered in most Biblical study courses. I just decided to jump right in.

"Your wife tells me that you haven't touched her vagina in over a year. Is that true?"

Here is where I expected him to clarify the misunderstanding and point out that this was not, in fact, the case. But no such defense was offered. He calmly admitted that what she told me was the truth. Upon further examination, I discovered he was up to his eyeballs in porn and was more interested in masturbation and a host of other disturbing activities rather than making love to his own gorgeous wife.

I just sat there stunned.

I would love to say that was the last time I ever heard such a sad story, but I would be lying. The truth is, I have heard multiple versions of this very same story over and over again. If there is one thing that seems true, it is this: Many men who grow up masturbating end up more comfortable with their own hands than of their wife's body. And that, my male, testosterone-infused, testicle-carrying friend is nothing short of an absolute travesty.

"But Pastor Mark, I've been masturbating every day since I was 13. What can I do?"

What can you do? You can stop.

"But I can't!"

Nonsense.

"But what about grace?"

Grace?? Sadly, many believers today have become convinced that grace is not empowerment, but permission. That since there is grace, it is pretty much OK to do anything they want. But that is a perversion of grace. Sounds more like "grease" to me.

Paul the Apostle wrote these words to his young friend Timothy:

> *For the grace of God has appeared that offers salvation to all people. It teaches us to say "No" to ungodliness and worldly passions, and to live self-controlled, upright and godly lives in this present age.*
>
> – Titus 2:11-12
>
> New International Version (NIV)

Did you catch that? Paul says the grace of God teaches us to say "No" and to control ourselves. And we can do it now, in this life, not just after we die. If your version of grace does not give you the ability to successfully say "No," you do not know what true grace is.

"But the Bible never says anything about masturbating!"

Really??

When talking specifically about sexual sin,

Jesus, in his sermon on the mount, said these words:

> *"I tell you that anyone who looks at a woman lustfully has already committed adultery with her in his heart. If your right eye causes you to stumble, gouge it out and throw it away. It is better for you to lose one part of your body than for your whole body to be thrown into hell. And if your right hand causes you to stumble, cut it off and throw it away."*
>
> – Matthew 5: 28-30
> New International Version (NIV)

What, exactly, do you think he was talking about when speaking of how one's "right hand" would cause a person to stumble? Picking their noses??

"But I've tried to quit! I can't control myself!!"

But Paul teaches that the grace of God can help you control yourself.

Come on guys! What are we saying here??

That we are like animals that are forced to act on pure instinct, without logic and without control? That self-control is beyond our capabilities? That despite our greatest efforts, little porn gnomes attack us and force us to stare at screens of naked women and grab our wieners while we cry out, "Stop! Stop!"??

"But I've asked God to take away these feelings..."

Ahhhh, NOW we are getting to it. You have been convinced that if you feel it, you must do it, but you could not be more mistaken. The great thing about God's power and grace is that it enables us so we DON'T have to do what we feel. That, unlike animals, our feelings do NOT determine our behavior. That at the end of the day, we simply choose. Period.

Look, the only way God could take away your "feelings" is to kill you. As long as you are alive in this sinful body, you will feel all kinds of bad things. The key to living as a victorious Christian, filled with God's Spirit and grace, is that we do

NOT have to do what we feel. And until you learn that lesson, you will be a victim your entire life.

You can stop. And you can stop today. No one forces you to masturbate. The very thought is patently absurd. Every time you masturbate, it is you choosing to do so – you are not forced by some invisible power. And when you do it, you are spilling your sexual energy for absolutely no reason. Ultimately, this behavior will rob your future wife of the passion you should be storing up for her.

And here is a final thought you should take very seriously – and this should affect any and all sexual behaviors: If you cannot learn to control yourself before you are married, you won't be able to do so *after* you are married.

Ever wonder why so many people cheat on their spouses *after* marriage? Because they never learned to say "No" *before* they married. All of their lives they simply have done what they felt. And when they feel like cheating – they cheat. They have always behaved that way.

You think bad, sexually immoral feelings

disappear after you marry? Think again. Till the day you die, life is filled with temptations. Learn the wonderful secret of a successful Christian life: We do NOT have to do what we feel. The grace of God teaches us to say "No." We don't have to wait till we die to be able to live a self-controlled life. We can do it right here, right now.

Until a man learns to be the master of his own penis, he will remain a slave.

The good news is: You can be free – starting today.

"So if the Son sets you free, you will be free indeed."

– John 8:36

New International Version (NIV)

POTENTIALLY NEGATIVE SIDE EFFECTS FROM MASTURBATION:

- Premature ejaculation when having actual sex

- Reduced testosterone levels

- Erectile Dysfunction

- Performance anxiety

- Chronic fatigue

- Insomnia

- Reduced sperm counts

- Socially withdrawn

- Depression

- Lack of mental focus

Chapter
Twelve

Make a Decision

Every time I meet a single woman I give her this advice: If he doesn't ask you to marry him by the end of 12 months... dump him! I particularly love giving this gem of advice right in front of the guy she is dating. The shock on his face is priceless.

The idea that a man needs more than twelve months of dating before being able to decide on marriage is patently absurd. Any serious-minded individual can decide within a year if they want to do life with a specific woman. In fact, you don't even need a full year, but certainly no longer.

This, of course, is blatant heresy to the

culture of "just take your time" (a culture I will strongly assault in the next chapter). The problem is that any dating couple – yes, even devout Christians – who get extremely close to each other are likely to become sexually involved if they date much past twelve months, if not before. Then you have the problems described in chapter nine. This is why serious dating before age 17 is a really bad idea. If you start seriously dating after turning 17 and truly fall in love with each other, you can go forward with marriage (as my wife and I did at the ages 19 and 18). But if you start seriously dating at 16, 15 or even earlier, you are virtually guaranteed to become sexually active with each other and bring on some potentially serious complications.

And I repeat: The idea that a couple needs more than twelve months of dating before being able to decide on marriage is patently absurd.

In his book, ***Kosher Sex,*** Rabbi Shmuley Boteach writes of how very conservative Jews approach marriage:

First, a man and a woman meet. They

do not necessarily know how attractive they will prove to each other. However, assuming that they meet and everything goes well, they continue to see each other for a period of time, say a few weeks or even a few months and then they decide on marriage.

This is how Hasidic Jews approach marriage even today. They assume people can make an intelligent decision even in a matter of weeks! And keep in mind that divorce in that culture is very rare.

After one year any intelligent adult can decide on whether or not they want to do life with another person. Besides, what is to be gained by delay? What magic do people think will set in after years and years of dating? The only likely "magic" that sets in after a long dating period is sexual activity that then makes the couple dumb as a brick. Best to make your decision in the light of day when everyone is thinking clearly.

And besides, why should a woman waste

years of her life dating some dude who can't make up his mind about her? This extended dating is robbing millions of young women of their most precious years, and for what exactly? Let me share with you what is currently happening to so many women today by men who can't make up their minds...

She is 20 years old. She dates some guy for five years. He then dumps her (for whatever reason). It takes her two years to recover. She is now 27.

She starts dating another self-centered narcissist. He also dates her for five years before he ingloriously dumps her and it takes her another two years to recover. She is now 34.

Once again, she jumps blindly into the dating pool, dates for another five years before being gloriously dumped once again. After her two-year recovery, she is now 41 – and wondering:

Where are all the available men?

Sadly, she has allowed indecisive men to rob her of her youth.

**DO NOT WASTE THE MOST
PRECIOUS YEARS A WOMAN
HAS WITH ENDLESS,
POINTLESS DATING!!**

**Be a man.
Grow a pair.
Make a decision.**

Chapter Thirteen

Tick, Tock, Tick, Tock...

If you are already an older, never-married single, this chapter could be a bit depressing for you. My intent, however, is not to make older singles feel bad. My intent is to warn the younger singles about the inherent dangers of delaying marriage till later in life.

Let me be clear: A lot of people marry later in life because, for whatever reason, they just cannot find someone they want to marry. I have no problem with that. The problem I have is with the current culture of deliberately delaying marriage for no better reason than an irrational fear of marrying too young.

The idea of what many consider is "too young" to marry is a relatively new phenomenon. As recently as 1970, the average age of a woman marrying was 20 years old. For thousands of years of human history, men and women married at 16 – 21 years of age. Most Biblical scholars believe that Mary was 14 when she gave birth to Jesus.

Now, I am not arguing for 14-year-old mothers, but the current trend of waiting till almost 30 years of age to marry is patently absurd. The problems created by delayed marriage are stunning both in number and severity.

I can understand a pagan culture that does not see the value of marriage and encourages sexual experimentation to push for later marriage. But I cannot, for the life of me, begin to understand how and why Christian leaders and parents have bought into this insanity. Sadly, they have been influenced more by secular reasoning than Biblical truth.

And you need to know that when secularists (who carry a decidedly anti-marriage point of view) site negative statistics concerning young marriage, many of their "facts" are based more on urban legend than in actual truth. They even cite the 50 percent divorce rate – which is total baloney. Looking at actual statistics, first time marriages in America have a divorce rate much closer to 15 – 20 percent, and certainly nowhere near the 50 percent mark. Yet the secularists continue to proclaim the 50 percent divorce rate as fact, but it is pure urban legend – a fantasy, and one that has succeeded in frightening a great many young people to stay away from the institution of marriage altogether.

And when secularists claim that young marrieds have a higher rate of divorce than those who wait to marry later, what they are not telling you is that the number they quote comes from very young teen marriages – even younger than 17. Then they tell you that later marriages (closer to 30) have a lower rate of divorce. What they don't tell you is the number they skipped over – the early twenties – this is the group that has the lowest rate of divorce. And studies have shown that there is little additional divorce-prevention benefit to marrying past ages 22 to 25.

But all of these skewed statistics miss the point. The real motive behind all this fact twisting is very simple: Hard-core secularists worship at the altar of money. They believe that the most important thing for a successful marriage is a secure financial state. But the absurdity of waiting for "enough money" is this: Exactly how much is enough? Who, but the 1 percent in the world have "enough money?" I'm in my sixties and fairly successful in my chosen field – more than most – and I still don't have "enough money." If I had "enough money," I probably wouldn't be sitting at this late hour, typing out this manuscript. I'd be relaxing on some beach in the Pacific. Quit worrying about "enough money." This money thing has gotten so far out of hand as to be utterly ridiculous.

Exactly how much money does one need to be married? And what happens if financial setbacks occur after marriage and the couple falls below that number? Should they now file for divorce and traumatize the children they brought into the world all because they fell below a certain number? Come on, if you need a certain number to get married it only stands to reason that you must maintain that number in order to stay married, right?

But the actual truth is that a successful marriage is not established or defined by money. In fact, studies have shown that the couples who have the greatest struggles in the beginning are often the ones who successfully build marriages that last for a life time – in other words, those who start with the least amount of money, education and security. And if couples with the greatest struggles have the most successful marriages, why do parents insist that their children remove all struggles before marriage?

Another absurdity I hear from singles is that they cannot afford to live together as husband and wife. This is beyond stupid. Seriously: Do the math. If single A can survive on his own and single B can survive on her own, what idiot came to the conclusion that A and B together now cannot survive? The truth is, it is less expensive for them to live together as husband and wife. One rent bill instead of two. One utility bill instead of two. One everything instead of two. Basic economics tells you that the economy of scale tilts dramatically in the favor of one married couple over the two singles.

And what exactly are Christians doing worshiping at the altar of money along with the pagan secularists anyway? Purity and morality should be much higher on our priority list than money. Yet I have had Christian mothers come up to me in churches and proclaim, "I would rather my kids have sex than marry too young." What kind of moral insanity is that?!? It is as if they are saying, "Who cares about offending the God of heaven – what really matters is that we don't offend the god of money."

"But what about college?"

What about it? Again, studies have shown that married college students perform better than their single counterparts – especially the men. They are finally getting sex on a regular basis and can actually think about something else for five minutes.

And as for the argument that marriage would be a distraction to young college attendees – this is utter nonsense. Marriage is not distracting. You know what is distracting? Dating!! The emotional ups and downs associated with dating are far more distracting than marriage. Hey, you wanna wait till after college to marry? Fine. But then don't date. Your constant dating will only distract you from your studies.

As I already stated, the problems created by delayed marriage are stunning both in number and severity. I want you to look at six of them with me...

1. Sexual Immorality

Many in the Christian community are alarmed at the rate of sexual immorality among our young people today. But rather than follow the Biblical solution...

But since sexual immorality is occurring, each man should have sexual

relations with his own wife, and each woman with her own husband.

– 1 Corinthians 7:2

...we look desperately for a program to make up the difference. Why? Because we don't really believe the Bible. We fear and discourage marriage for the young rather than encourage it. As a result, we invent ineffective programs like the Promise Ring – a ritual where young men and women pledge themselves to a life of sexual purity until marriage. **The problem is:** It doesn't work. Studies have shown that those who take purity pledges have the same rate of pre-marital sex as those who do not, once they enter college.

We ignore the Biblical answer – marriage – because we have been convinced by a sick and broken pagan culture that the worst possible thing is to marry young, a position that is wholly unsupported by the facts. If the Biblical answer to sexual immorality is marriage and we discourage young marriage, then we are by default encouraging sexual immorality.

2. Porn Addictions

If, by some fluke, we are actually successful in convincing our young men not to have intercourse with their girlfriends, we are then left with incredibly frustrated young men. Since so many reject the teachings of scripture to marry as a solution for sexual frustration or temptation, the next logical step, it would seem, is the temporary relief of masturbation. A very troubling behavior that I have already discussed in detail in Chapter Ten.

3. Eunuchs

Here is one you probably never heard about: Creating eunuchs (essentially). Again, for those who don't know what the word means, it means a man without testicles. Very wealthy men of old, especially kings, would hire eunuchs to take care of their households. Why a eunuch? Because the master of the house never had to worry about the guy being inappropriate with his wife or daughters. Since he had no testicles, the man could not produce the necessary testosterone to so much as cause an erection.

I fear that we are creating a version of eunuchs today with this foolish obsession to delay marriage. This is what happens: We tell young men not to marry young, but also not to have sex. So, he tells his body for 20 years (age 13 to 33), No, No, No, No, No. He successfully represses every sexual urge that he has (all while being applauded by well-intentioned, but misguided, pastors and parents) to the point that he has little to no interest in sex by the time he does marry.

I first noticed this during a tour in South Africa. South Africa is a beautiful country, filled with some of the most wonderful and amazing people. By and large their churches, in my opinion, are more spiritual, energetic and effective than any American church. But these fabulous people have a big flaw in their thinking: They encourage delayed marriage to almost absurd levels. Wait for money, wait for maturity (which we will discuss next), pay a dowry (an absurd pagan tradition that has had terribly negative results in delaying marriage and creating sexual sin), wait for the approval of parents. By the way, I had one South African pastor tell me, "But we do this to win the families to Jesus." Really?? You mean the Jesus who said...

> "Do not suppose that I have come to bring peace to the earth. I did not come to bring peace, but a sword. For I have come to turn a man against his father, a daughter against her mother, a daughter-in-law against her mother-in-law
>
> – Matthew 10:33-35

But I digress...

So, I had a young lady at one of my seminars in South Africa approach me with a very stern look on her face. She was not a happy girl. She grabbed me and said, "We did everything right! We waited and waited and waited – we were both virgins. Finally married at 35...and now I just about have to RAPE him to get him to have sex with me!!"

And what really stunned me was the fact that I had heard this complaint multiple times during my tour. It didn't take long before I started hearing this same complaint in the U.S. It finally dawned on me, "Good grief – by encouraging these men to shut down their sex drives till 30 plus years of age, we have foolishly created our own unique version of a eunuch." Because it would appear that after years of shutting down their sex drives, they cannot jump start them later when they marry.

To be clear: This does not happen to all men who delay marriage, but it happens to far too many. From my experience, ending up as a 40-year-old virgin is generally not a good idea for a man.

4. Delayed Maturity

Then we have the utter foolishness of thinking that twenty-something boys are just too immature for marriage. Sadly, what these proponents of delayed marriage fail to see is that it is not age that matures men – it is marriage and responsibility.

In an article that appeared on January 27, 2008, in the ***Dallas Morning News***, Kay Hymowitz wrote:

> *For whatever reason, adolescence appears to be the young man's default state, proving what anthropologists have discovered in cultures everywhere: it is marriage and children that turn boys into men.*

Military commanders all over the world have witnessed this transformation for thousands of years. Take a young boy, impose discipline and lay upon him life and death responsibility and he transforms quickly into a man. The military proves every day that you can take an 18-year-old boy, and in a matter of months, have him operating multi-million dollar pieces of equipment flawlessly – equipment that millions of lives depend on. Anyone who has ever encountered a typical 19-year-old compared to a 19-year-old member of the military knows they are not looking at the same person. The former frequently remains immature, hoping mom will continue to cover his failings, playing video games and arriving late for work, while the latter is a responsible, respectful, confident young man.

It is not age that matures a boy into a man – it is marriage and responsibility.

The big complaint I get from young single women is that there are no responsible, mature, single men available. Of course not – all the guys they are looking at haven't had to become responsible!! And if we are being totally honest here, many young women find themselves admiring (or worse – attracted to) married men. Why? Because they are so much more mature!! What they fail to realize is that he is mature for only one reason: He is married.

5. Fertility Problems

There are so many women in their 30s and 40s who are praying desperately that they get pregnant. Their hearts are broken, asking God why they haven't been able to conceive. Why? I'll tell you why – because your body does not care that you wanted to wait for your career and money and parental approval before you married.

Research, by Dr. Tom Kelsey at University of St. Andrews and Dr. Hamish Wallace at University of Edinburgh, provides evidence that women are born with a fixed number of eggs and that number declines with increasing age. Every time a woman has her period she loses one of her eggs. Every month. One after another, after another. Their study showed that for 95 percent of women, by the age of 30, only 12 percent of their eggs remain, and by age 40 only 3 percent are left. Fertility experts also note that the older the eggs, the more difficult they are to fertilize.

And would somebody explain the logic here? Everyone is waiting to have money BEFORE they get married. Then, since they delayed so long, they cannot conceive – so they spend countless THOUSANDS OF DOLLARS trying to get pregnant! And what was the win here??

Not only do we have less children, those very same children are at a considerably higher risk for complications. The risk of having a child with a birth defect caused by missing, damaged, or extra chromosomes is increased in older women. This is especially true in children conceived by in vitro fertilization.

According to a 2006 article published by the *Daily Mail* and written by Fiona MaCrae, a mother's age at the time of her baby's birth is connected to the longevity of her offspring:

> *The secret of a long and healthy life could be as simple as your mother's age at the time of your birth. Babies born to women under 25 are almost twice as likely to live to 100 as those born to older mothers, a study has shown.*

And it's not just the woman. Science is showing that men also have a biological clock. Amy Sohn of the *Wall Street Journal* wrote:

> *Now...another study (this one in the journal "Nature") has shown an association between older fathers and schizophrenia, autism, and bipolar disorder in their offspring.*

To be clear again: These things do not happen to all older parents. The elevated risk, however, is very real. But it would seem that, rather than do the obvious and sensible thing – encourage young marriage and young families – we get advice like this from a *USA Today* article quoting Dr. William Schoolcraft:

> *"I think it's going to change how men view reproduction. If they are really serious about having a family, they may put away a couple of sperm samples as an insurance policy so if it is later in life when they conceive, they have the option of using that young sperm which is probably going to give them healthier babies."*

Really? Delay marriage at all costs and even freeze your sperm? For the love of...

Let's forget about personal heartbreaks for a moment: Western culture is experiencing a severe demographic crisis. We are literally breeding ourselves out of existence. And we are the first generation of Christians to begin self-elimination due to low birth rates.

Most Western cultures are now below the replacement rate for their citizens. Meanwhile, Muslim couples are having six to eight children per family. Do the math. What do you think the world is going to look like fifty years from now?

6. The Elimination of Grandparents

And finally we get to this one: The elimination of grandparents.

For thousands of years of human history, it has been the presence of loving and caring grandparents that has been the major stabilizing factor in human families. Even in our present time, social workers will tell you that it is often the grandparents that make up the difference in the lives of their grandchildren if their parents struggle or divorce.

For thousands of years, men and women became grandparents in their 40s and 50s. Deb and I became grandparents in our 40s. We now have six. And as any grandparent can tell you, the presence of these grandchildren is the single greatest joy of life. These are men and women who have experienced most everything that the world has to offer, yet they will testify with absolute certainty that their life's greatest joy is their grandchildren.

Well, if you are like most millennials today, you will likely never experience that joy in its fullness. Think about it: If you are 35 when you have your first child and your offspring does the same – you will be 70 years old before that first grandchild appears. And by the time you can have an intelligent conversation with them, you will be in your 80s (ignoring the fact that statistically you will already be dead). In your 80s you won't have the emotional, physical or financial energy to play a meaningful role in that child's developing life. And if mom and dad fail – there won't be anyone to pick up the pieces. And mark my words: There will be hell to pay in society when we have succeeded in eliminating grandparents from the equation. The state will have to step in and what a disaster that will be.

According to an AARP study:

▶ 53 percent of grandparents contribute to educational costs

▶ 37 percent contribute for everyday living expenses

▶ 27 percent contribute for medical or dental costs

▶ 16 percent provide daycare services

▶ 11 percent are actually raising their grandchildren

▶ 78 percent discuss religious or moral values with them

▶ 37 percent discuss sex and dating with them

▶ 47 percent take their grandchildren to religious services

According to the study, "...today's grandparents contribute to the basic quality of their grandchildren's lives; they are the safety net for American families, helping to pay for practical expenses and necessities."

And the millennial generation is going to lose all of that for what? So they can delay marriage for as long as possible? So they can be obsessed by trying to amass all the meaningless toys of life? "Delay, delay, delay," is their mantra. And their number one goal: make sure they are financially, educationally and emotionally secure before they marry – as if there is any guarantee they could succeed at that anyway.

For being a supposedly "well-educated" lot, they seem to have a problem doing basic math. Many will still have kids in school when they reach their 60s – forget about being meaningful grandparents to their children and grandchildren. Many seem ignorant of the fact that life spans end at about 78 for most Americans. Even with great advances in medicine, that is not likely to change all that dramatically. I tell 39-year-olds who still can't get serious about their marital status, "For heaven's sake – you are half dead!" Their response? They just stare. They have never thought about it. They think they have forever. They don't think of the many negative consequences they risk by refusing to grow up and move on. And lest you think I am laying the blame of this foolishness on the millennial generation, I am not. I blame their parents. Men and women who have their priorities completely out of whack and passing their twisted values on to their kids. Men and women who have been fooled into believing "facts" that are not facts at all. Men and women, who themselves have been so obsessed with money, that they pass their materialistic obsessions on to their kids. And I'm talking about Christian parents.

I must now repeat the first two paragraphs of this chapter...

If you are already an older, never married single, this chapter could be a bit depressing for you. My intent, however, is not to make older singles feel bad. My intent is to warn the younger ones about the inherent dangers of delaying marriage till later in life.

Let me be clear: A lot of people marry later in life because, for whatever reason, they just cannot find someone they want to marry. I have no problem with that. The problem I have is with the current culture of deliberately delaying marriage for no better reason than an irrational fear of marrying too young.

Chapter
Fourteen

The Older Single

Assuming that you are not totally depressed by now from reading about the importance of marriage at a young age, there is still good news for the older single. You can still find someone to love you and do life with you. But you must be realistic.

1) Don't wait for "God to send you someone" – go look!

2) Depending on your age, children may be out of the picture. That is okay. The good news is that even though children are important,

127

they are NOT the central purpose for marriage. And, of course, there is always the option of adoption. There are children out there who desperately need parents.

Don't dismiss this as an option. They don't need to be from your womb in order for you to truly love and cherish them.

3) You may likely find someone who already has children (perhaps you do as well) – whether divorced or widowed – and that can be a MAJOR problem. Remember, at this stage in life you are likely joining someone who has already had a life. It can be tricky, but it can be done. Think it through. Be intentional. There may be ex-spouses to deal with, adult children to deal with, ex in-laws to deal with, etc. etc. etc.

4) Be forewarned: Things progress really quickly when you are older. Don't think you can date for as long as you did when you were young. You will need to be very

intentional and make decisions very quickly or you will soon find yourself among the throngs of the mentally numb because pre-marital sex made you stupid.

Enjoy the life you have. And for heaven's sake, be as intentional as you can. The clock never stops ticking...

Chapter
Fifteen

Conclusion

In the ocean of information (or misinformation as is often the case) on dating, it's easy to see how so many people end up "lost at sea" while trying to navigate their way to matrimony. And in all honesty, many well-meaning and good-intentioned pastors, leaders, teachers, and experts – as well as loving friends and family members – give misguided advice that only serves to push those seeking a wife further off course and adrift.

"But how can so many Christian leaders be wrong about all this?"

Well, that's the problem, isn't it? It

is precisely because so many well-meaning and highly respected people have repeated misinformation that we just accept it as truth. But inaccurate and misguided information never becomes truth just because someone we respect repeats it. And oftentimes, misinformation is taken as truth for no other reason than because it is repeated at all – never mind who repeats it. For example, ask most people how many wise men were in the Christmas account and almost every single one will answer: Three. But nowhere in the Bible does it say how many there were. People just automatically believe it was three since for years we have heard the Christmas carol, "*We three kings of Orient are...*"

And don't just believe me. Look at the scriptures for yourself. You will find that there is little to no evidence that God will bring you a spouse or that he has ordained a soulmate for you or that he will tell you whom to marry. What you will see is that marriage always has been and always will be a choice. **Choose wisely.**

While there is no magic formula, what we

have explored in the pages of this book are certainly very helpful guidelines that will empower you to make wise, intentional decisions that will facilitate the process of finding a woman of good character. Someone you can successfully do life with.

If you will put aside all the less-than-helpful information you've learned along the way from your friends, discard Hollywood's version of dating and romance, reexamine the over-spiritualized input from the Christian community that lacks Biblical foundation and employ the principles I've outlined, you will be able to think clearly and make a good decision so you are not just driven towards some disaster in response to some primal urge to wed.

Think it through.

Be intentional.

Stop over complicating it.

Stop over-spiritualizing it.

Find the girl.

More Books by Mark Gungor

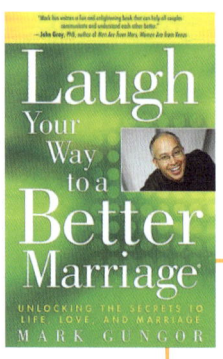

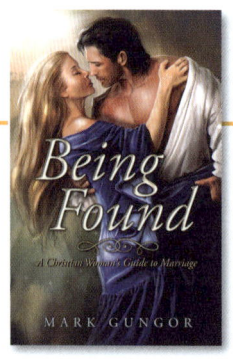

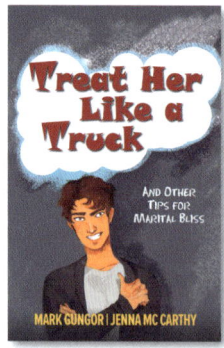

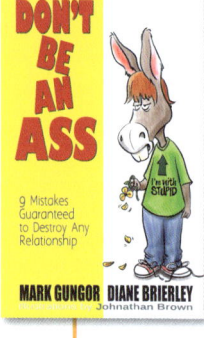

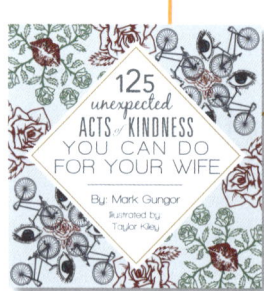

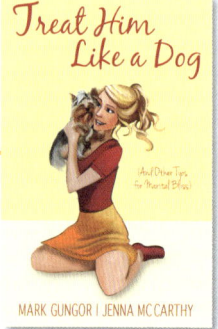